Grandpa,
~ tell me ~
your story

SPECIAL NOTE

Dear customers,

Thank you for your trust.

I'm an independent publisher.

If you like this journal, feel free to follow my

work on my website : www.olindavida.com

so you don't miss any update.

I hope you will enjoy this journal as much as I

enjoyed designing it !

Erika Rossi
- Ô LINDA VIDA -

Dear grandpa,

I offer you this diary so that you can give me the greatest gift : the gift of your life story and experience.

I know and love the person you are today through your role as a grandfather, but I would also like to discover your other facets and the different phases that have marked your life and made you the man you are today.

All you have to do is give me back this diary filled with your most personal thoughts, anecdotes and memories. You can either fill it out with me or do it on your own.

Feel free to skip any question you don't want to answer. They have been thought of to guide your life testimony, and can be completed with your own reflections at the end of the diary and embellished with your most beautiful pictures!

Once you have finished your story, I will keep this memory book carefully, a priceless treasure that can be passed on to our descendants.

I hope you will take as much pleasure in filling it out as I will in reading it.

Thank you very much

♡

Summary

YOU

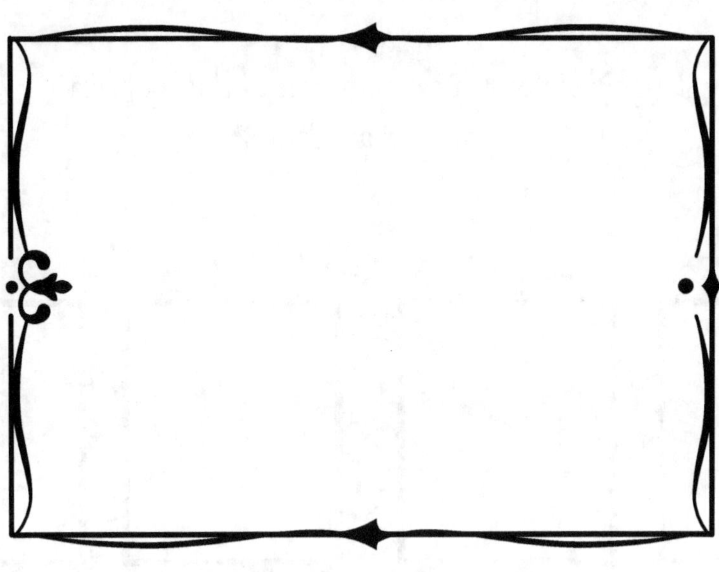

Your name is

....

How did your parents choose your name ?

....

....

Today; ...., you have .... children, ...
grandchildren and .... great
grandchildren .

You were born on .... in ....

YOUR ROOTS

*(Complete with the names and dates of birth
of your ancestors)*

Our best picture ♡

YOUR YOUTH

Did you like going to school ? Did you do well or was it hard for you ?

What were your favorite and least favorite subjects ? Are there any subjects that don't exist anymore ?

Who were your best friends ? What are your best
memories with them ?

When you misbehaved, how were you punished ? How often
were you punished ?

As a child, what was the job you wanted to do when you grew up ?

What were your favorite games/toys ?
How did you spend your free time ?

How did your parents describe you ?

Did you have pets ? If not, do you wish you had ?

What was your nickname ? Why did they call you that ?

What did you do during school vacation ?
If you went away, who did you go with and where ?

What was the biggest mistake you made as a child ?

What was your favorite book ?

What was your favorite food ? What was your least favorite food ?

Tell me the funniest memory of your childhood.

Which birthday is your most special memory ?

Did you have any special family traditions ? What were the family celebrations like and which ones did you prefer ?

What are the happiest memories of your childhood ?

A picture of you as a child ♡

A picture of you as a child ♡

As a teenager, what did you do with your friends ? Did you go out a lot? Did you keep your childhood friends ?

Overall, did you enjoy your adolescence ? What are your best memories ?

Une photo de toi adolescent   ♡

 YOUR FAMILY

Tell me about your parents : what were their jobs ? Describe their habits and their respective characters. What memories do you have with them ?

Your mom :

Your dad :

A picture of your parents ♡

What did your grandparents do and what were they like ? How often did you see them ? What did you like to do with them or at their house ? Did they teach you anything ?

A picture of your maternal grandparents ♡

A picture of your paternal grandparents ♡

What do you know about your great-grandparents and more distant ancestors ?
Does our family have a particular ethnic background ? Are there any stories/legends about our ancestors' bloodline ?

If you have brothers and sisters, what are their names ?
What is your relationship with them like ? Are there any
memorable stories about them ?

Where did you live with your family and what was your home like ?

A picture of your whole family ♡

YOUR ADULTHOOD

As a young adult, what were your best skills ? Which were you best at ?

What principles passed on by your parents have guided your adult life ?

What jobs did you have ? Did you enjoy them ? If you could have started over, would you have chosen the same work ?

Have you ever been on a long journey ? Where did you travel ? What are your favorite travel memories ?

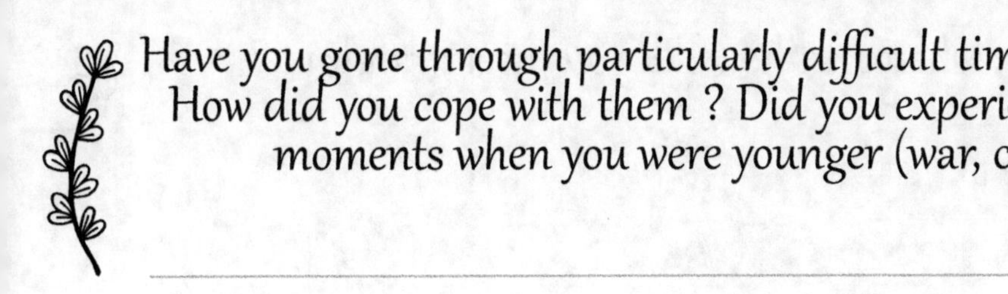

Have you gone through particularly difficult times in your life ?
How did you cope with them ? Did you experience historical
moments when you were younger (war, crisis...) ?

Tell me more about her.

How many serious relationships did you have before you met grandma ? What can you tell me about them ?

How did you know that your relationship with grandma was really special ?

What was your wedding like ?
Did you go on honeymoon afterwards ?

How did you decide to have a child ?

A picture of both of you ♡

At what age did you get your driver's licence ? And your first car? Do you have a funny story about it ?

What is the best gift you have ever received ?

Have you participated in any contests or competitions in your life ?

How has your perception and experience of masculinity evolved over the years ? What makes you feel like a "man" today ?

YOUR LIFE AS A DAD

How did you react when you found out grandma was
pregnant ? What about her ?

What was her first pregnancy like ? What about childbirth ?
How did you live them ?

How did you balance your family life and work obligations ?
If you could have started over, would you have done it the
same way ?

How did you choose your children's names ? Do they have a particular meaning? What were your other favorite names ?

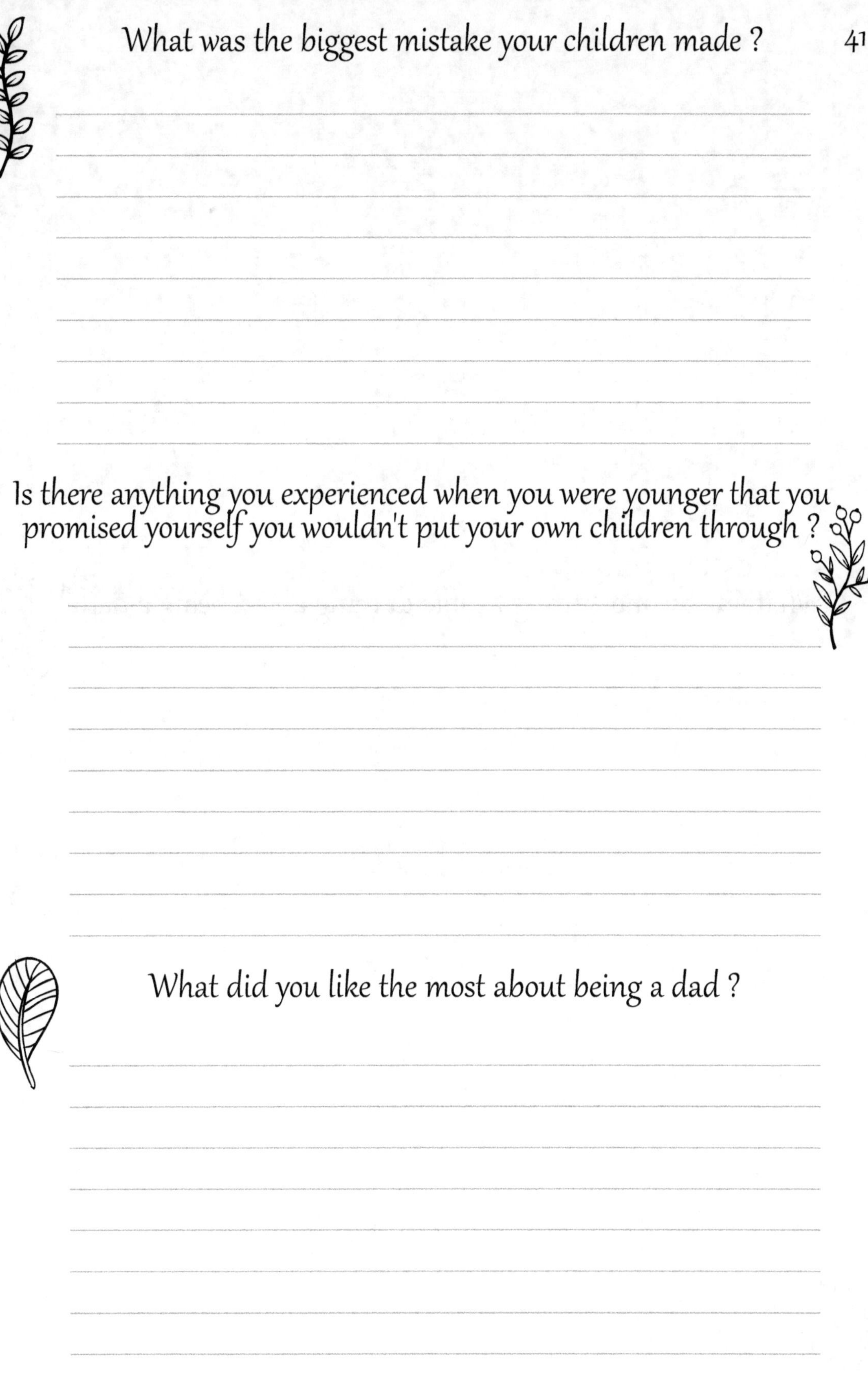

What was the biggest mistake your children made ?

Is there anything you experienced when you were younger that you promised yourself you wouldn't put your own children through ?

What did you like the most about being a dad ?

What was the most tiring / difficult thing about being a dad ?

What is your best memory with your children ?

Family pictures ♡

YOUR LIFE AS A GRANDPA

How did you feel when you found out you were going to be a grandfather?

What is your favorite part of being a grandfather?

Are there things about me that remind me of you ? Do we have anything in common ?

Is there anything you've always wanted to tell me ?

What are your favorite activities to do with your grandchildren ?

What are your most beautiful memories with me ?

Pictures of us ♡

YOUR CURRENT LIFE

What are your current favorite activities ?

What are your daily rituals ?

Describe our family in three words.

Is there anything I don't know about you that would surprise me ?

What are your favorite movies and actors ?

What are your favorite music styles and singers ?

If you won the lottery tomorrow, what would you do ?
(You can let your imagination run wild !)

What would you do if you only had one day left to live ?

According to you, what are the inventions that have most revolutionized the course of humankind ?

You and your relatives now ♡

RETROSPECTIVE OF YOUR LIFE

Where did you like living the most and why ? Would you have liked to live somewhere else ?

Do you think the world has changed a lot since you were born ? What has surprised you the most ?

Throughout your life, who have been your different role models or, a source of inspiration for you (relatives or celebrities) ?

What are you most proud of ? What experiences have been the most important in your life and have made you the person you are today ?

Do you have any regrets ? Do you wish you had done things differently ? What do you wish you had spent less time on ? What about more time on ?

What dreams have you achieved ? Are there any particular things you would like to accomplish ?

How do you imagine your retirement ? If you are already retired, what do you prefer in this phase of your life ?

What would you like to be remembered for ? What values are most important to you ? What legacy would you like to leave ?

What advice would you give me regarding my personal and professional life ?

I'D ALSO LIKE TO KNOW...

Your favorite tips & recipes

Your favorite tips & recipes

Your favorite tips & recipes

Your favorite tips & recipes

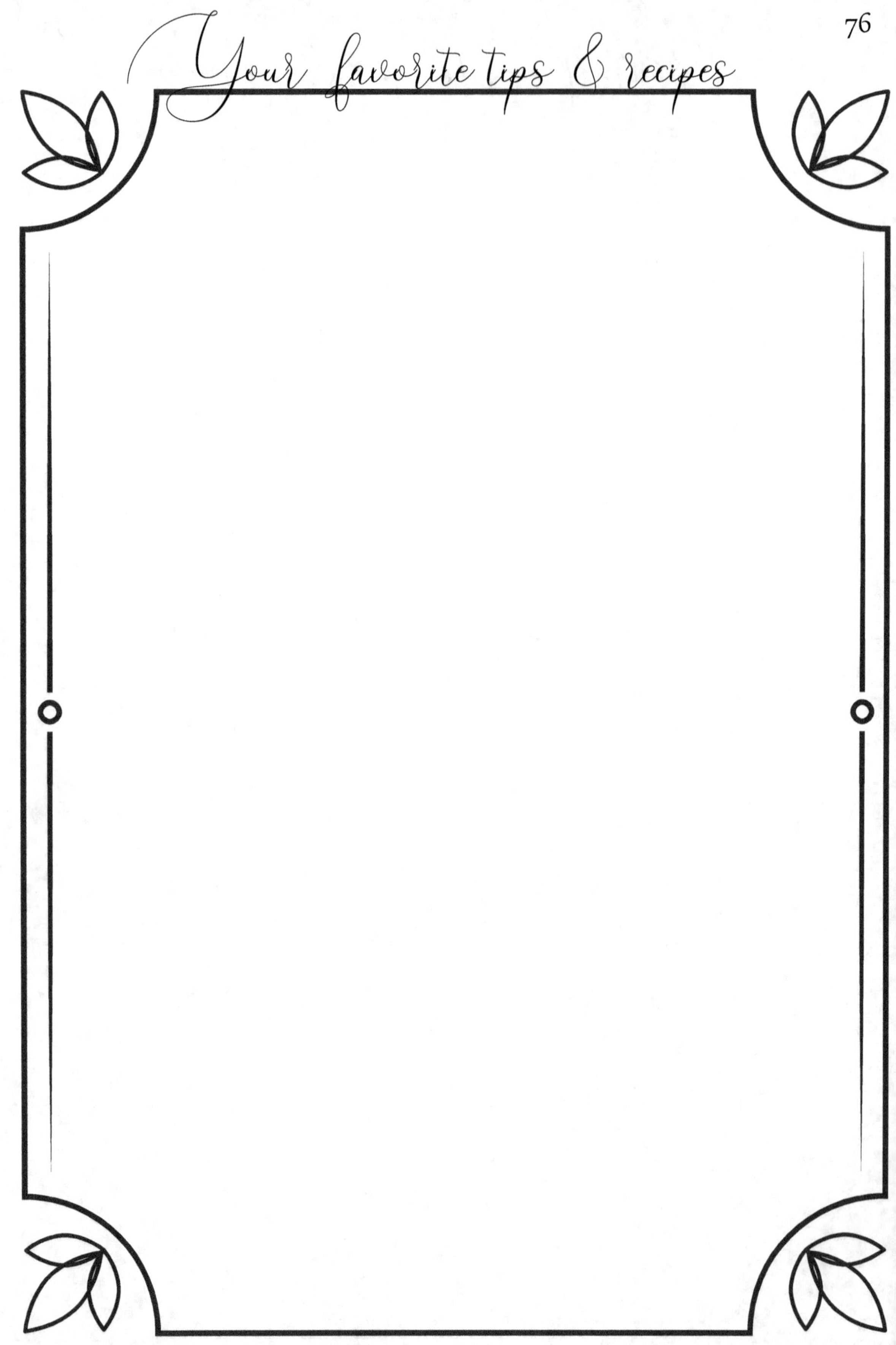

Your favorite tips & recipes

Your favorite tips & recipes

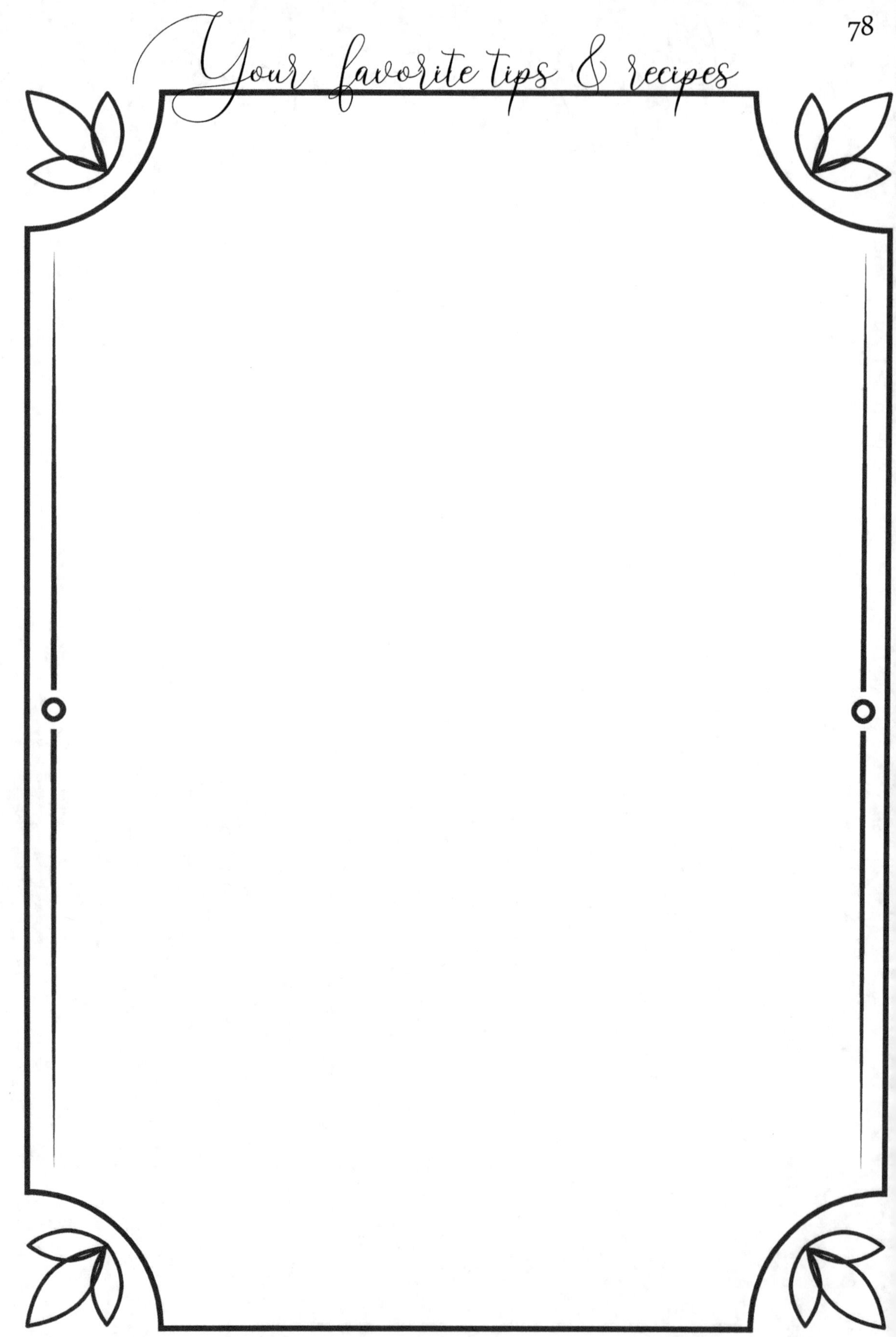
Your favorite tips & recipes

A little love note ...

From me to you :

From you to me :

Your life in pictures ♡

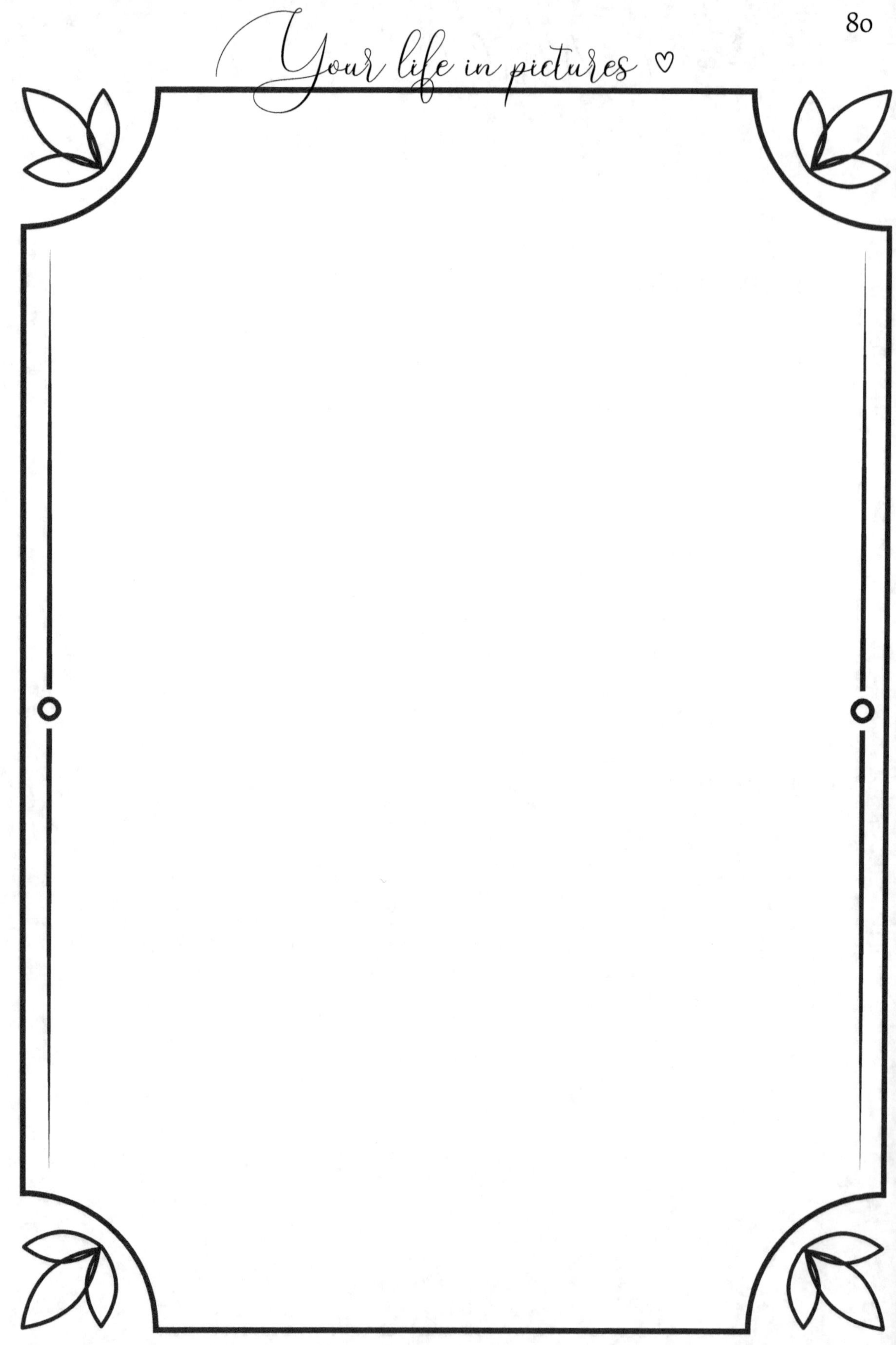

Your life in pictures ♡

Your life in pictures ♡

Your life in pictures ♡

Your life in pictures ♡

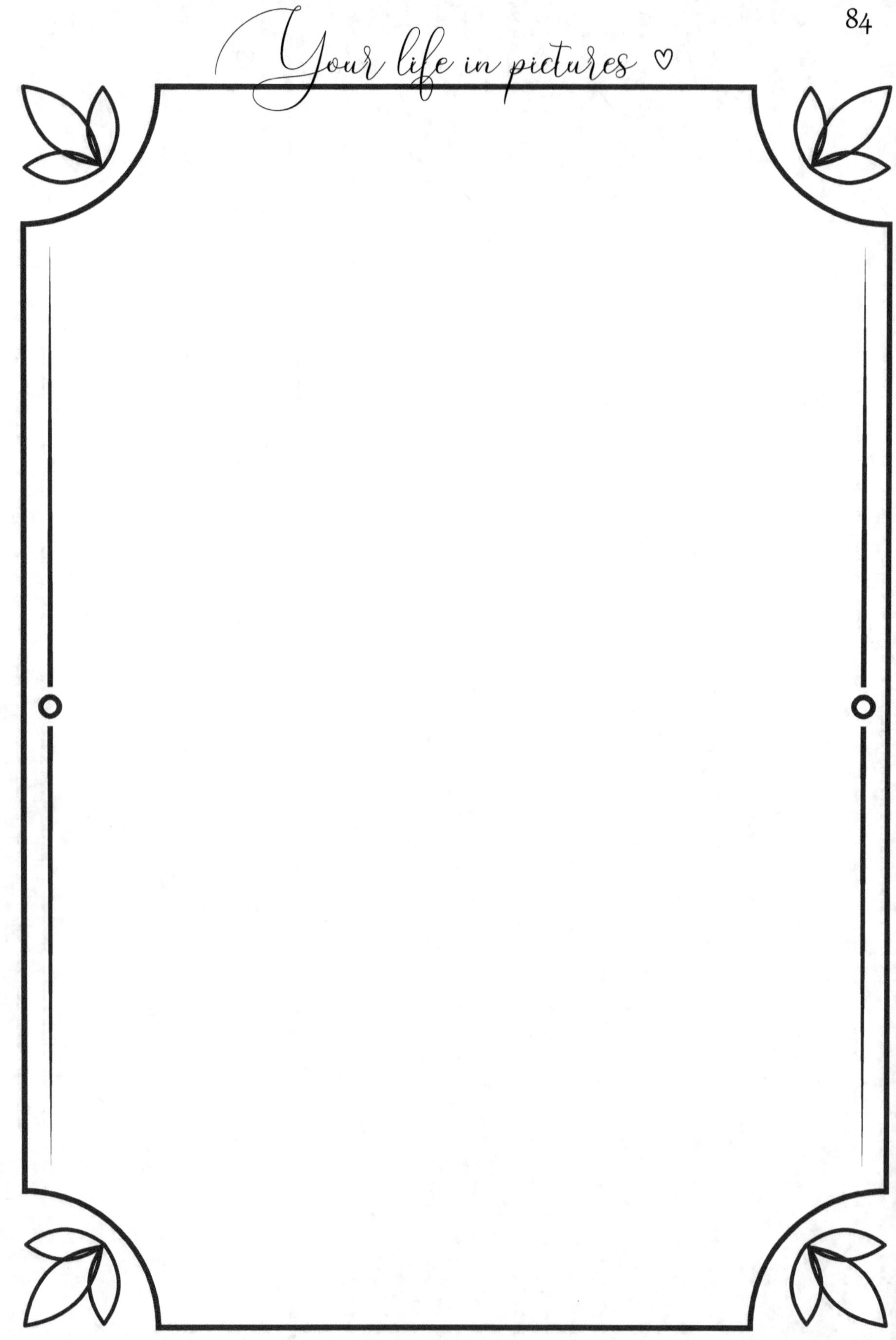

Your life in pictures ♡

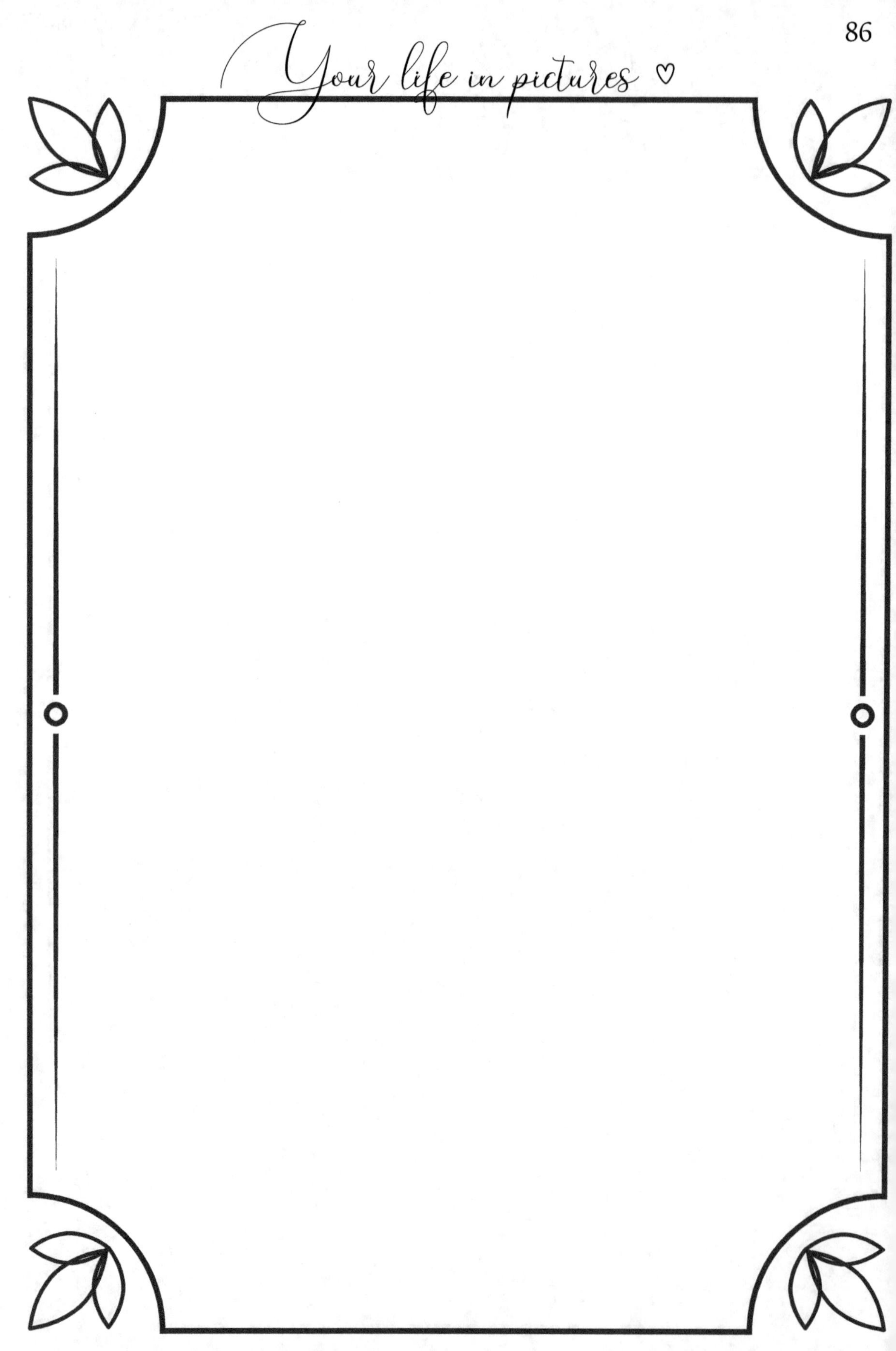
Your life in pictures ♡

Your life in pictures ♡

Your life in pictures ♡

Your life in pictures ♡

Your life in pictures ♡

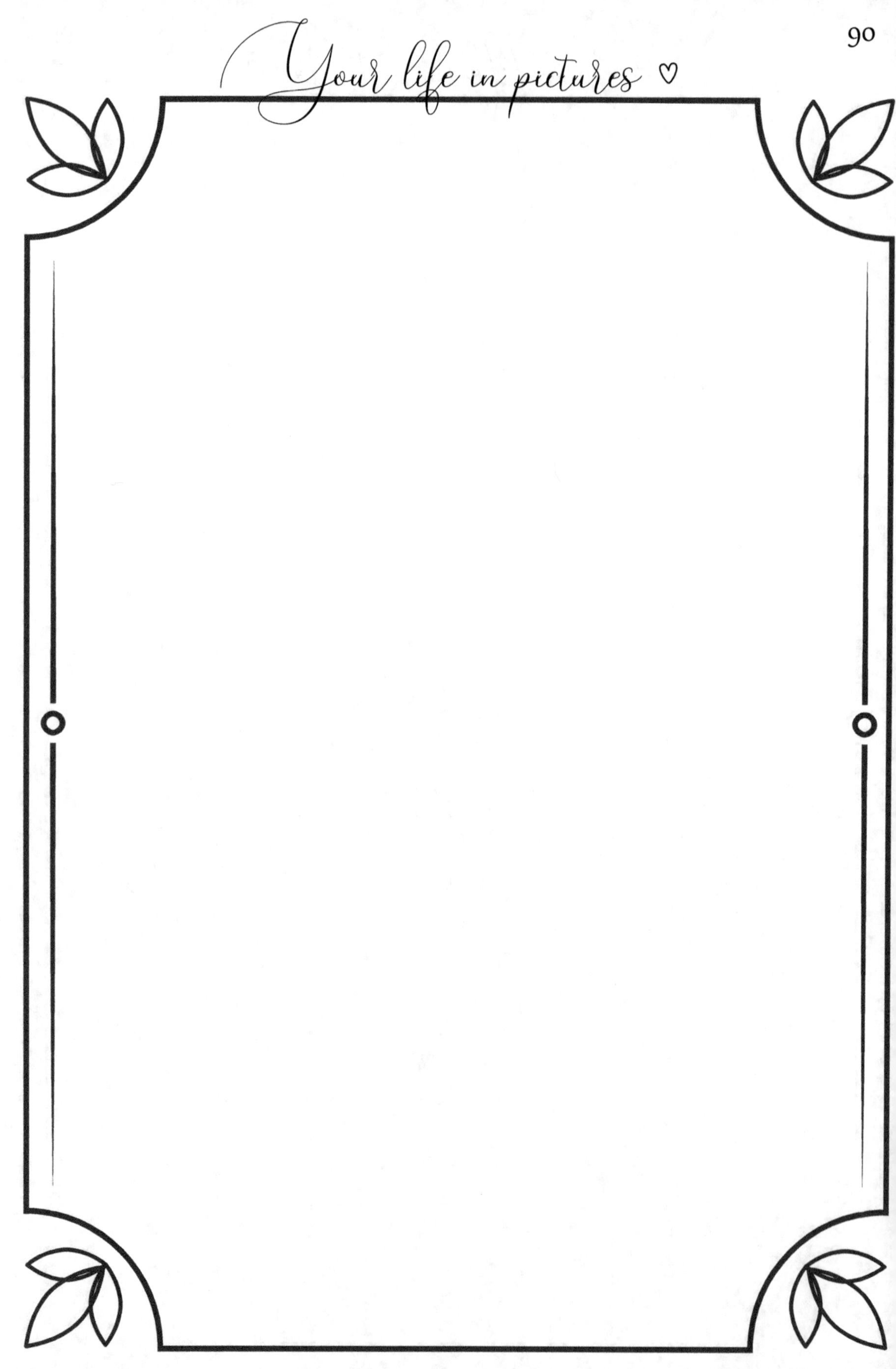

Your life in pictures ♡

Your life in pictures ♡

Your life in pictures ♡

Your life in pictures ♡

Your life in pictures ♡

EXTRA NOTES